Questions and Answers: Countries

Syria

A Question and Answer Book

by Mary Englar

Consultant:
Christopher Rose
Outreach and Study Abroad Coordinator
Center for Middle Eastern Studies
The University of Texas at Austin

Capstone press
Mankato, Minnesota

Fact Finders is published by Capstone Press
151 Good Counsel Drive, P.O. Box 669, Mankato, Minnesota 56002
www.capstonepress.com

Library of Congress Cataloging-in-Publication Data
Englar, Mary.
    Syria : a question and answer book / by Mary Englar ; consultant, Christopher Rose.
    p. cm. —(Questions and answers. Countries)
    Summary: "Describes the geography, history, economy, and culture of Syria in a
question-and-answer format"—Provided by publisher.
    Includes bibliographical references and index.
    ISBN–13: 978–0–7368–6412–1 (hardcover)
    ISBN–10: 0–7368–6412–1 (hardcover)
    1. Syria—Juvenile literature. I. Title. II. Series: Fact finders. Questions and answers.
Countries.
DS93.E54 2007
956.91—dc22   2006005058

Editorial Credits
Silver Editions, editorial, design, and production; Kia Adams, set designer; Ortelius Design,
    Inc., cartographer; Jo Miller, photo researcher; Scott Thoms, photo editor

Photo Credits
AP/Wide World Photos/Bassem Tellawi, 25; Sana, 9
Art Directors/Chris Rennie, cover (background); Michael Good, 12, 13
Corbis/Bettman, 7; K.M. Westermann, 21
Getty Images Inc./AFP/Awad Awad, 23; AFP/Joseph Barrak, 8; AFP/Karim Jaafar, 19;
    AFP/Ramzi Haidar, 27; Allsport/Tony Duffy, 18
One Mile Up, Inc., 29 (flag)
Photo Courtesy of Paul Baker, 29 (coins)
Photo Courtesy of Richard Sutherland, 29 (bill)
Richard T. Nowitz, 1, 6, 11, 15, 17
Shutterstock/Rebecca Picard, 24; Risteski Goce, 16
SuperStock/age fotostock, 4
Wolfgang Kaehler, cover (foreground)

1 2 3 4 5 6 11 10 09 08 07 06

Table of Contents

Features

Where is Syria?

Syria is in the Middle East. It's a little larger than the U.S. state of North Dakota.

Syria has a coastline of 120 miles (193 kilometers) along the Mediterranean Sea. There the summers are warm and humid. The plains along the coast have good farmland. Mountains divide the plains from the dry land of eastern Syria.

The northern countryside of Syria is good for farming.

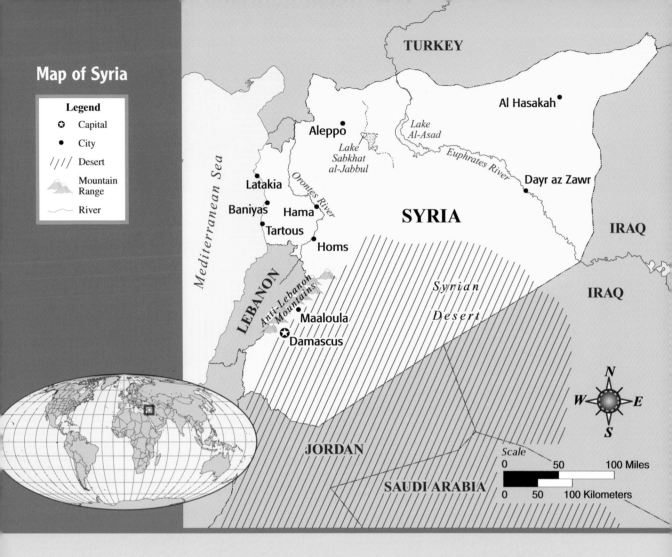

Map of Syria

Legend
- ✪ Capital
- • City
- //// Desert
- Mountain Range
- ~ River

TURKEY

Al Hasakah •

Lake Al-Asad

Aleppo •

Lake Sabkhat al-Jabbul

Euphrates River

Latakia

Orontes River

SYRIA

Dayr az Zawr •

Baniyas • Hama •

IRAQ

Tartous •

Homs •

LEBANON

Syrian Desert

IRAQ

Anti-Lebanon Mountains

Maaloula •

✪ Damascus

Mediterranean Sea

N
W — E
S

JORDAN

Scale
0   50   100 Miles
0   50   100 Kilometers

SAUDI ARABIA

Much of southern Syria is a rocky desert. The Syrian Desert covers parts of Iraq, Jordan, and Saudi Arabia. It has little plant or animal life. Freshwater springs in **oases** provide some water for farmers and shepherds.

5

When did Syria become a country?

Syria became a country in 1946. For 400 years, Syria had been part of the Ottoman **Empire**. When World War I (1914–1918) began in Europe, the Ottomans joined the Germans. They fought against the **Allied Powers**.

Syria joined the Allies to fight for freedom from the Ottomans. The Ottomans lost the war, and the Allies divided up the empire. In 1920, France took over Syria.

Fact!

The ancient city of Palmyra was an oasis in the Syrian desert. It was an important stop on trade routes more than 2,000 years ago.

Syrian President Tajaddin al-Husayni inspects French troops in 1941.

During the French **occupation**, a Syrian government was in place. But the French exercised much power over the government. Most Syrians resented French interference in their country. Fighting occurred off and on for 20 years. Finally, Syria won its independence in 1946.

What type of government does Syria have?

Syria is a **republic**. Since 1963, the Ba'ath party has ruled the country. Hafiz al-Asad served as president for 30 years. In 2000, his son, Bashar al-Asad, became president.

Syrian presidents have much power. They choose the two vice presidents and the **prime minister**. The president also makes new laws and is head of the Syrian army.

Fact!

When Syrian men reach age 18, they must serve 30 months in the military.

President Bashar al-Asad greets members of the Ba'ath party at a meeting in Damascus.

Every four years, Syrians vote for **representatives** to the People's Council. The Council can approve the president's new laws, but it cannot make laws. They meet three times a year in the parliament building in the capital city of Damascus.

What kind of housing does Syria have?

In Syrian cities, most people live in apartments. Wealthier Syrians live in the **suburbs** in single-family homes.

In rural areas, many people live in traditional homes. These houses have high ceilings and are made with mud brick. Most are built around an open courtyard.

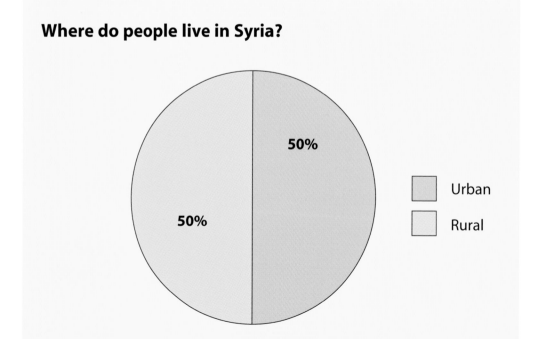

Where do people live in Syria?

50%

50%

Urban

Rural

The thick mud walls of beehive homes keep the inside cool during the summer.

In northern Syria, traditional houses have a cone-shaped roof and look like beehives. These homes are made of mud and straw.

What are Syria's forms of transportation?

Syrian cities have many forms of transportation. Streets in Damascus are filled with cars, buses, bicycles, and minibuses. Some farmers use donkey carts to bring produce to the market.

Fact!

In the past, some Syrians crossed the desert on camels. The desert people are called Bedouin. Today, most Bedouin travel by truck.

School children cross in back of colorful buses on a busy Damascus street.

Syria has good roads between its major cities. In small towns, many people depend on buses to go from place to place.

Syria has three major ports, Tartous, Baniyas, and Latakia. These ports are important centers of trade.

What are Syria's major industries?

Many Syrians are farmers. They grow cotton, wheat, and vegetables. The coastal plain and river valleys are best for farming. In the rest of Syria, farming is difficult. Not enough rain falls to water the crops.

Syrians also work in **industry**. Workers pump oil from wells in the desert. Textile factories make clothing from cotton, wool, and silk. Syrian factories also process dried fruits and meat.

What does Syria import and export?

Imports	Exports
food and animals	clothing
machinery	cotton fiber
metal products	fruits and vegetables
plastics	oil
yarn	wheat

Many colorful fabrics, used to make clothes, come from silkscreen workshops in the ancient city of Aleppo.

The service industry is also very important in Syria. People in the service industry work in government, education, and tourism. Tourists visit Syria's many historic cities, forts, castles, and **mosques**.

What is school like in Syria?

Most children in Syria start school at age 6. They must stay in school for at least six years. Most elementary students study either French or English. They also learn Arabic, math, science, and religion. Secondary school in Syria lasts six years.

Fact!

In 2002, President Bashar al-Asad created the first virtual university in Syria. Students can study on the Internet to get degrees from foreign universities.

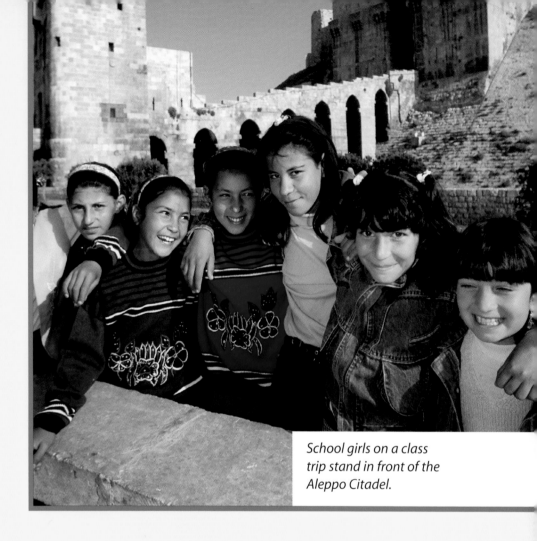

School girls on a class trip stand in front of the Aleppo Citadel.

Some students do not go to secondary school. These children must help at home. Some girls help their parents care for younger children. In small villages, girls sometimes get married before they finish school.

What are Syria's favorite sports and games?

Syrians love to play and watch soccer. The national soccer team plays against other Arab countries. Children play soccer in the parks and at school.

Basketball is almost as popular. Syria has a men's national basketball team.

Fact!

Ghada Shouaa won the first Olympic gold medal for Syria in 1996 in the women's heptathlon. This event includes the shot put, high jump, long jump, and a hurdles race.

Syria, in green, plays Qatar in the Emir Cup in 2005.

Many Syrian men go to cafes to watch soccer games between city teams. The city teams play against each other for a national championship. Men sip coffee and play backgammon as they watch the games. Backgammon and chess are very popular board games.

What are the traditional art forms in Syria?

Music is played everywhere in Syria. Clarinet players, drummers, and players of the **oud** perform at weddings, at parties, and in concerts. Often, a singer joins the musicians.

Syria is home to a special group of dancers called whirling dervishes. In the past, these dancers performed in mosques as a way to communicate with God. Today, whirling dervishes also perform at concerts and in restaurants.

Fact!

Damascus swords became famous about 1,000 years ago. These swords could cut a silk scarf in half before it fell to the ground.

Whirling dervishes perform spinning dances in traditional long, white skirts.

Damascus is known around the world for its fine cloths. Textile workers embroider silk cloth with flowers and other designs. This silk fabric is called damask, because it is made in Damascus.

What major holidays do people in Syria celebrate?

Syrians celebrate Independence Day on April 17. This day celebrates the country's independence from France. Syrians have the day off. In the evening, Syrians watch fireworks. Children eat candy and ice cream.

Some Syrians celebrate Christian holidays such as Christmas and Easter. Many Syrian Christians live near Damascus in the village of Maaloula.

What other holidays do people in Syria celebrate?

Eid al-Adha
Martyr's Day
Muhammad's Birthday
New Year's Day

People wave Syrian flags during Syrian Independence Day.

Most Syrians celebrate **Muslim** holidays.
During the month of Ramadan, Muslims do
not eat or drink between dawn and sunset.
At the end of Ramadan, Muslims celebrate
Eid al-Fitr. Families buy new clothes, cook
special foods, and visit relatives.

23

What are the traditional foods of Syria?

Syrian meals often begin with appetizers called mezze. Mezze dishes can be olives, cheeses, pickled vegetables, or dips made from eggplant or chickpeas.

Main dishes often include grilled lamb or chicken. Cooks sometimes serve stewed meat over rice. Dishes are flavored with many spices, such as garlic, cumin, and pepper.

Fact!

Many Syrians eat a breakfast of pita bread, yogurt, string cheese, olives, and cucumber slices. Breakfast can also include bread, jelly, and melons.

A variety of pastries are available during Eid al-Fitr, the end of the Ramadan fast.

There are many fresh fruits available in Syria. Grapes, melons, dates, and oranges grow well in Syria's climate.

In large cities like Damascus, families often take walks after dinner. They might stop for ice cream or sweet pastries.

What is family life like in Syria?

Most Syrians have large families. Grandparents, parents, and children often live together in small apartments. Young adults usually live at home until they marry.

Many men in Syria have more than one job. Women traditionally stayed at home, but now more women have jobs to help support their families.

What are the ethnic backgrounds of people in Syria?

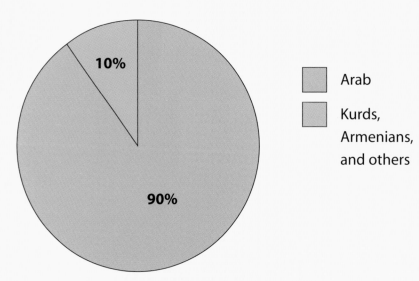

10%

90%

Arab

Kurds, Armenians, and others

Families often celebrate holidays together with large feasts.

On farms, every member of the family has to do work. Some years, there is not enough water for the crops. Then, farmers cannot pay their bills. Young people often move to the cities to find jobs. They send extra money home to their parents.

Syria Fast Facts

Official name:

Syrian Arab Republic

Land area:

71,062 square miles
(184,050 square kilometers)

**Average annual
precipitation:**

9 inches (23 centimeters)

**Average
January temperature
(Damascus):**

44 degrees Fahrenheit
(7 degrees Celsius)

**Average July temperature
(Damascus):**

81 degrees Fahrenheit
(27 degrees Celsius)

Population:

18,448,752

Capital city:

Damascus

Languages:

Arabic (official), Kurdish,
Armenian, Aramaic

Natural resources:

asphalt, chrome, gypsum,
iron ore, manganese, oil,
phosphates, rock salt

Religions:

Muslim	90%
Christian	10%

Money and Flag

Money:

Syria's money is the Syrian pound. In 2006, 1 U.S. dollar equaled 52 Syrian pounds. One Canadian dollar equaled 46 Syrian pounds.

Flag:

The Syrian flag is red, white, and black. The red represents the struggle for freedom, white represents peace, and black represents the past under colonial rule. The two green stars represent Syria and Egypt. From 1958–1961, the two countries joined together to form the United Arab Republic.

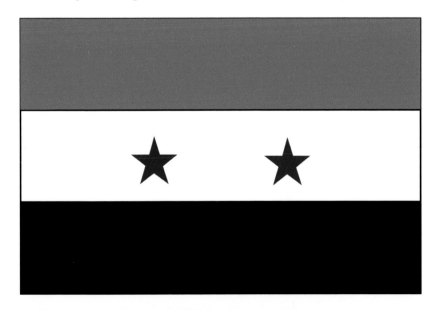

Learn to Speak Arabic

Most people in Syria speak Arabic. It is the official language of Syria. Learn to speak some Arabic words using the chart below.

English	Arabic	Pronunciation
hello	marhaba	mar-HAH-bah
good-bye	ma'assalama	MAH-sa-lah-ma
please	min fadlak	MIN FAD-lak
thank you	shukran	SHUK-ran
yes	na'am	NAHM

Glossary

Allied Powers (AL-ide POU-urs)—group of countries that fought together in World War I. Some of the Allies were the United States, England, France, Greece, and Italy.

empire (EM-pire)—group of countries that have the same ruler

industry (IN-duh-stree)—a single branch of business or trade

mosque (MOSK)—a building used by Muslims for worship

Muslim (MUHZ-luhm)—a person who follows the religion of Islam; Islam is a religion whose followers believe in one god, Allah, and that Muhammad is his prophet.

oasis (oh-AY-siss)—a place in the desert where there is water; plants and trees grow in oases.

occupation (ok-yuh-PAY-shuhn)—taking over and controlling another country with an army

oud (OOD)—a string instrument with a pear-shaped body that is similar to a guitar

prime minister (PRIME MIN-uh-stur)—the leader of a parliament, a government body that makes laws

representative (rep-ri-ZEN-tuh-tiv)—someone who is elected to speak for others in government

republic (ree-PUHB-lik)—a government with officials elected by the people

suburb (SUHB-urb)—a town near the edge of a city

Internet Sites

FactHound offers a safe, fun way to find Internet sites related to this book. All of the sites on FactHound have been researched by our staff.

Here's how:
1. Visit *www.facthound.com*
2. Choose your grade level.
3. Type in this book ID **0736864121** for age-appropriate sites. You may also browse subjects by clicking on letters, or by clicking on pictures and words.
4. Click on the **Fetch It** button.

FactHound will fetch the best sites for you!

Read More

Behnke, Alison. *Syria in Pictures.* Visual Geography Series. Minneapolis, MN: Lerner Publications, Co., 2005.

Draper, Allison Stark. A *Historical Atlas of Syria.* Historical Atlases of South Asia, Central Asia, and the Middle East. New York: Rosen Pub., 2004.

Gnojewski, Carol. *Ramadan: A Muslim Time of Fasting, Prayer, and Celebration.* Finding out about Holidays. Berkeley Heights, NJ: Enslow Publishers, 2004.

Tay, Alan. *Welcome to Syria.* Welcome to My Country. Milwaukee, Wis.: Gareth Stevens Publishing, 2005.

Index